Tales From the Farmlands

Tales From the Farmlands
Samantha Nicklaus

This is a book of poems. Any resemblance to actual persons, living or dead, or actual events is purely coincidental.

No portion of this book used Artificial Intelligence in any way, shape, or form. No portion of this book can be used to teach, train, or otherwise engage with any AI in any capacity.

Reviews can be left on Amazon.com or GoodReads.com

Cover art by Kati Karloff

PURPLE SUN

To the family I've found along the way.

Contents

Introduction

I wanted the hurt out of me. I gave myself a week, one week, to write an entire poetry book. I want the hurt out of me. Rush through the pain, the sad, the grief– and then be done with it. Quick as lightning, quick as a flash. But this wasn't a rain drop; this is a whole hurricane. I've been writing this book for months and the hurt is still there. Just when I think it's gone, I find it hiding under the stairs. The hurt is constantly moving, like the goalposts I cannot live up to. If this isn't my bloodletting, I don't know what is. Slowly draining, draining, draining and maybe if I live through it, you'll finally consider me strong. Strong, as if I am not pulling every punch. Even now. The hurt is still there and I want it out of me. I wish this didn't hurt.

The Troll that Lives Under my Brain

Silver spoon, born under a half-moon,

But still not immune to the monsoon.

Power hour with a champagne shower,

Can't see the view from the golden tower.

The pain from the chain is a part of the campaign,

But in the same vein, it's an easy reign.

Your creator is a dictator,

A professional retaliator

You were cut, and for what?

A nut with a haircut?

A prime crime, another rhyme,

Lemons and limes, but never teatime.

Stay a while on this isle,

We have a lifestyle of exile.

A lonely daughter sent to the slaughter,

The rotters wash away in the floodwater.

A smack (but take it back) on the fast-track.

The wolf pack sees no set back, just a snack.

Broken free and absentee,

Try to solve my riddle three.

Egyptology

Nile crocodiles, Antony, and papyrus scripts—

An ancient history, but a present empire.

Hieroglyphics etched into stone, with

Historians spending lifetimes trying to connect the dots,

Looking to decipher the secrets

Hidden in plain sight, there for anyone to see,

Legible, but impossible to understand.

How do you capture the vernacular of the time,

How do you translate slang or pop culture?

A reference to an event there is no record of?

Artifacts of the past entombed with their owners,

Carefully curated, a museum dedicated to a lifetime,

Stone doors sealed tight, an immaculate resting place,

But sometimes, sometimes the living get locked

in with the dead and what becomes of them?

Dying in a gilded tomb, a pretty brutal death.

Those locked out will cry, will lament how they

Aren't a part of the spectacle that is decomposition

But when the grave robbers find the bodies,

Decades or centuries later,

When they find the gold and the relics and the jewels,

The story will be pieced together and will become

one of love, one of mourning.

It would take a lifetime to comb through the truth,

And another one to understand it.

Nuance is difficult to translate.

You Are What You Eat

Snake in the grass,

A hidden danger looming

Like a black cloud on the horizon.

An ever present after thought,

Even after St. Patrick has been to town;

The threat is unforgettable and undeniable.

Did you know you can be bitten by a snake,

But not be envenomated?

The original evil can pull punches.

The sign of a liar, a betrayer, a conman;

You can't say you didn't know when you picked it up.

A snake is a snake is a snake.

Imagine my surprise when I look in the mirror

And see the slit of snake eyes looking back at me.

How could I forget; you are what you eat.

Anniversary

It was January fifth the first time

You said "I love you" and meant it.

Like the current in a river, it nearly swept

Us both off our feet.

You had said it to me before,

When you wanted to mean it, but couldn't.

This time it was real.

This time you said "I love you"

And you meant it with a sincerity,

A truth that can only be found on a molecular level.

It felt like coming home.

History is Written by the Victors

An olive branch in my outstretch hand

Slows down time, a second stretch across an eternity.

For a brief moment, the branch becomes a bridge

Connecting two lost souls together.

It makes the slap to the face that much more cruel.

With the imprint of the branches on my cheek,

I am unprepared but not shocked.

This was never a war and you are not the enemy.

I thought you an ally, and now… you are nothing.

Any battles you see are illusions,

Any reference to you, a misinterpretation.

The nostalgia of you is no longer strong enough

to keep you afloat in the ocean you put between us.

You chose to drown and I cannot save you.

I still wish you well, but to call you

Insignificant would give you too much credit.

I cannot meet you in the middle of a no man's land

Filled with bombs bearing your name.

I have left the trenches and gone home.

I'm sorry if you stay there, waiting

for a fight that will not come.

There is no treaty to be made, no peace to be brokered.

The shrapnel in my heart is a constant

reminder of what it is like to trust you.

I have no more fight in me.

You may call it a victory if you wish,

But your name won't be written

in my history book's footnotes.

Work in Progress

On the outskirts of the farm, there are

Wolves of all shapes and sizes.

Deep in the woods, if you look carefully,

You can see the bear traps meant for them.

Wolves are a threat to the farm,

And threats must be dealt with.

If they are caught in a trap, it is not uncommon

For a wolf to chew off its own leg to escape.

Can you imagine the survival instinct?

The dedication and love of life?

Do you think they curse the monster who set the trap,

Or the trap itself for their pain?

If the farmer stepped into his own trap,

Do you think the wolves would start with his leg?

Surely you cannot expect compassion

When your prey turns predator.

I have seen many bear traps.

I have not seen many three-legged wolves.

Imagination

I have always had a strong imagination,

A sense of wonder and whimsy,

that no one could ever take away,

for better or for worse.

When I was small, I lived in my imagination.

Now, the landscape is the same, but the

Plot to the stories looks different.

In my make believe, you are sad.

In my make believe, you repent

With tears in your eyes, you fall to your knees,

"Dear God, what have I done?"

In my make believe, you care.

And when I dream, sometimes I see you.

Or the you my brain has created,

Where your foul words sting less when you say them,

Where I do not have to appease or apologize,

And in my dreams, I can find a million ways to

Explain to you the hurt you have caused.

In reality, no combination of words could sway you

And I know better than to try– deaf ears and all that.

In reality, I was too inconsequential

to even cross your mind.

And please don't do that,

Don't wrap obligation in a cloak and call it love.

I know where reality ends and make believe begins;

I know it's a dream when I can fly,

And I know it's make believe when you apologize.

Conversion

I was a non-believer before you,

A sinner lost in a sea of false gods and lackluster idols.

Like a prophet, silver lined words

Slid off your tongue and turned me into a believer.

Atheist turned devotee,

I'll receive your blessings when you offer them.

Anoint me with holy oil, let me glow

under your biblical light.

Your tongue speaks the word of god—

Of the only god worth believing in,

And I would never let myself be called heretical again.

Let me worship you in the church of your own making,

The walls you build of wood and stone,

Make a fine place to pray.

Your lips on mine is the only baptism I need,

Your hands in mine is the only heaven I believe in.

The mountains of past turn to ant hills at your touch.

Water into wine is child's play compared to

The way you transform doubt into certainty.

I cannot help but to drop to my knees and pray.

Down the Rabbit Hole

When Alice fell down the rabbit hole,

do you think her mother cried?

Do you think she ran through

the house, screaming "Alice?"

She would have checked the garden,

frantic and focused.

And Alice would be nowhere to be found.

And when Alice came back, do you think

her mother cried again?

Held her daughter close, face buried in her hair,

A silent sob of relief wracking through her.

Do you think her mother pulled away,

Confused and worried,

When Alice answered the question

"Where have you been?"

How did her mother take the answer?

Did she reassure Alice it was all

just a dream, despite the protests?

Did she let her believe it was real?

What did she say when Alice yearned to go back?

And when Alice sees the Cheshire cat in the garden,

And starts speaking to the rose bushes,

And asks the field mice if they would like some tea,

What did Alice's mother do?

How do you love someone who lives in Wonderland?

The River, Again.

The River of Time has softened the knife

you left in my back into a precious stone

I can run my fingertips across the softened edge now,

With no fear of bloodshed.

I worry about speaking life into your ghost;

summoning spirits is not something I'm familiar with.

I'm worried if I touch the memory, it will pop

like a bubble or dissipate like a magician's smoke screen.

I was taught to never speak ill of the dead

but I'm not sure what to do when the dead rise again.

The sun gives us life, but the moon gives us love.

I think of you at night, in the safety of the darkness,

In the serene silences, the echoes of you ring clear.

When I look up at the stars, I wonder if you do too.

I would return your knife if I could only find you.

Staring at the Sun

I've never found a battle I wouldn't fight,

So if you want to see who blinks first,

I wish you the best of luck.

Actions speak louder than words, huh?

You would kill to see your ideals brought to fruition,

But I would die to see mine.

If Isaac Newton stood on the shoulders of giants,

I have stood on wasted potential and casual cruelty.

You wanted to be left alone, so don't you dare

Look this gift horse in the mouth.

If you want to be judged on your actions,

It's not my fault the verdict came back guilty.

My delusions about bettering the world may

Weigh heavy on my shoulders, but your illusions

of grandeur are in a completely different weight class.

I threw every line I could think of, said every word,

Danced every jig, drew every comparison.

But fuck me, I will not blink first.

I will die staring into the sun.

Static

You think me a picture frame,

But I am a TV screen.

The list of factoids you have are

Long outdated, but you cling to them still

The sign in the museum was updated,

The Wikipedia page was changed,

But you were never a big reader.

I learned about confirmation basis in college,

Unknowingly your favorite trap to set.

I worry if I go missing, you couldn't

Describe me to the police.

I wonder; would you call the police?

And isn't that sad?

A tragedy, really, but I'm the only one to cry.

A Shakespearian villain, unable

To read the lines on the page.

Sick animals will bite, but the dead ones can't.

Cremated, buried, embalmed?

I bet you couldn't guess.

Better yet, you will guess this is about you.

I'm ashamed to say I saw it coming, but didn't move.

A tsunami wave in the distance, and I

Watched it from the shoreline.

There is a saying about one bad apple

Ruining the bunch.

Uneducated, unempathetic, and unabsolved

I grew up on Old Yeller so I know

A rabid dog when I see one.

It's sad you don't believe in vaccines.

Scalpel

How do I take the you out of me?

You are in my eyes and the way I laugh,

My muscles can't help but write my "J's" just like you.

My subconscious became a trophy on your mantel,

Another prize in your collection that

Will gather dusts like all of the rest.

How can I take the you out of me when I am *you*?

If I cut you out, what would be left of me?

Every strand of DNA is another piece of you.

You are my worst fear; I am what you could have been.

If I could rearrange your atoms, move your

thoughts into a different order–

We are the same deck, but different hands.

There are more combinations in a card deck

Than stars in the sky, but no matter how

I shuffle; we are no closer to matching.

And still, I can't take the you out of me.

Me and Daddy Are Different

Originally written at age 10

Me and Daddy are different,

We just can't get along.

He is tall, I am short.

He has no hair, I have lots.

He says "prrnt" and I say point,

He likes football, I don't.

He drives a car, I don't.

I go to school, he doesn't.

I do homework while he does the bills.

He likes politics, I don't.

I like dolls, he does not.

I like cats, he doesn't.

(He thinks that cats taste like chicken, when he

Hasn't even tried one)

He reads the paper while I read the comics,

He worries about the electric bill, I don't.

I have to worry about how my hair looks in the morning,

He does not (he doesn't have to worry about that at all!)

He thinks I take too long in the shower, I don't.

I think he is bald, he does not.

I think stuffed animals are cute, he does not.

I think the news is boring, he does not.

Wait! Stop the press!

I thought of something we can agree on!

We love each other!

Tales From the Farmlands

You were born here, screaming and ready,

Your inheritance a puppy and a cleared acre.

Time moves on, but the land stays still and steady

You will die on this land, buried by the local undertaker

It is well known that we reap what we sow.

The dark dirt you crawl through tastes like metal,

The soil is soaked with a sour blood flow.

Don't run too far, the field is surrounded by nettle

Your family has owned this forever, this farmland,

The sacrifice of your ancestors is something to appreciate

The story of your family, summarized by a cattle brand

Did you think you were handed a clean slate?

When the moon is gone and the earth is salted with tears

The farmland becomes something you fear.

The Shape of Dyslexia

I can never see the trees through the forest,

And apparently that is diagnoseable now.

When I see words, I see them like ⬜

The only math I was ever good at was geometry,

Because reading to me is just shapes.

⬜ and ⬜ and ⬜ and–

Can you see the difference?

Hand me a pen and I can write you

a word with no vowels,

A mystery only I could solve.

Pieces of the misshapen puzzle forced together

because I cannot match them.

How many zeros are in ⬜ ?

Every string of numbers a

mystery, every new word a riddle.

Sound out ?

I can guess based on the shape,

but I will see more syllables

Than astronomers see stars in the sky.

Letters have never danced for me,

Or maybe they have and I could not see.

How do you read words you cannot see?

The answer is very well, apparently.

The author who cannot see letters,

Needs many editors indeed.

Mother of Two

The bridges I've burned don't light the way,

They illuminate the darkness.

The monsters in the stories are real

and they know who their friends are.

I have carefully groomed my Rage into a fine villain.

I will not leave her behind;

I have worked hard to grow her,

And I cradle her close to my chest.

My rage has grown big and strong,

And her big sister Hope is right behind her,

Present and hungry.

The bridges I've burned were not so you could not cross—

It's so my children could not get to you.

I'd hate to see you maimed.

Good Dogs Bite

The dogs on the farm are tools,

Like a tractor or hoe or sprinkler.

The guard dog guards and

The herding dog herds.

A working dog is a happy dog.

And when the guard dog goes after the chickens,

It is a sad accident, nothing more.

And when the herding dog chases the sheep off,

It is a training issue, nothing more.

Wide eyes and smiles assure you nothing is wrong.

The guard dog fights off bears and the

Herding dog returns the flock safely,

And you know all is well on the farm.

It's cute when the herding dog nips at you heels too,

And who can blame the guard dog for growling?

You were too close to see it.

You were too close when you got bit.

You were too close when you were attacked.

Now the dogs are covered in blood and you wonder

If you have failed the dogs or the dogs have failed you—

But the answer doesn't matter.

The blood is red and warm and the dogs want more.

Locksmith

I invented a time machine

That I can never use.

Take three steps backwards,

Spin around six times, and sit on the ground.

You'll find a key, a simple house key,

A lock in the back of your neck, right

at the base of your skull.

Turn the key and let the ooze drip out.

Let the brain and blood and time and love

Be slowly pulled asunder.

We need to unlearn to go back,

To forget and bury.

Rip the stitches out by hand, if you have to.

You can go back, but the price is hefty.

You can go back, but you may not recognize yourself.

You can go back, but you may hate yourself.

If you decide to travel backwards,

Please don't write.

I don't need the reminder of what is behind me.

I cannot take the heartbreak a second time.

Every road leads to Rome, after all.

My fate was written into my bones,

No matter what I chose to do,

I will always end up on this side of the aisle.

Just because I know how to turn back

Doesn't mean I will, but somedays,

I hear the echoes of laughter, and I understand why

Orpheus turned around.

I understand, but I am locked on my path forward.

I'm sorry you refused to keep up.

Genetics

If I wanted to list the things wrong with me, I wouldn't
know where to start. I collect medical problems like
trading cards. I grind my teeth so loudly in my sleep that I
can be heard through doors. Somehow, I am always too
loud. I have a great internal clock, but consistent
delusions of how much I can accomplish in five minutes.
I chew on the inside of my cheeks. I have to focus on
listening to other people because I get too excited for my
turn to talk. My hair sheds like a husky. I have rarely had
a thought that isn't shared. I need at least three
medications to keep me alive. I tell people I will watch the
show they recommend, just to go home and watch the
same shows over and over and over again. Sometimes,
my neck makes me go temporarily blind. I was nearly
twenty-two before I learned that not everyone argues
recreationally. I am allergic to mint and gravity.

I have never found an ill I wouldn't wish on an enemy
and I have never encountered a consequence I wouldn't
bear. There isn't a hill I won't die on. Better yet, I haven't
found a hill I won't kill you on.

Two Ships in the Night

She says we could have fallen

In love. I agree with her but

It's a lie. I have love for so many,

And she is included in that,

But in the back of my mind

I picture the world ending,

And there is only one person I

Would search for. In my

Final moments, it's always him.

And I'm sorry to those who

Expected more of me and

From me. I never lied but

I was never fully honest.

It was always him.

A Quick Wish List

I hope my great-great-great grandkids learn what an atom is made of and where the galaxy ends.

I hope, generations from now, they know that the point of humanity, the only reason we can survive, is our collective strength.

I hope that they explore the stars with the same fascination and love I feel when I look up at them.

I hope they always feel loved.

I hope they visit museums and read every sign.

I hope when they smile, it is with their whole face, not just a curl of their lips.

I hope they look back on the cruelty of humanity, they are disgusted and know to do better.

I hope they never lose hope.

I hope they think of me, however long ago, thinking of the future with them in it, and know that someone long ago thought of them fondly.

Little Dandy Lion

When I was little, I was told a

Dandelion was a weed, something

To pull out of the grass, to remove.

Yellow like the sun, if you waited for it,

You could use this weed to grant a wish.

Still, it was nothing more than a weed.

A weed, a weed, a weed.

I stopped picking dandelions as a grown up,

I was too big to believe in wishes, too

Jaded to care about picking weeds.

Until I saw a little girl in the park making

A crown out of bright yellow weeds.

I went to pick a dandelion too,

And it whispered "flower" to me.

Now, all I am surrounded by flowers.

Flowers, flowers, flowers.

A Little on the Nose

The snake oil salesmen took up residences in our home,

Both invited and welcomed with open arms.

We all knew of fool's gold, but

How do you scratch test a person?

The salesmen's eyes lingered a bit too long,

On the fine china, on the backdoor, on our little sister.

But he sat at the head of the dining room table.

While the neighbors point and laugh, you

Point right back, and the snake oil salesman disappears,

But only for a moment.

I haven't seen our neighbor in a moment.

The local lake has turned black,

And the town is full of child-sized graves.

I thought it ignorance, but I'm learning its malicious;

An intellectual with a backbone of steal–

I'm embarrassed I thought that of you.

The cruelty was the point, the end goal,

Your crowning achievement.

I'll take the prose out of it so you stand a chance of
understanding me: you are an embarrassment to the
values you claim to hold dear.

No, No Thank You.

No thank you to the people who tell me being a full-time author is impossible. No thank you to the people who were supposed to show up for me, and didn't. No thank you to people who wear their lack of empathy as a badge of honor. No thank you to anyone who tries to shame me for resting. No thank you to people who only ask how I am to leverage that information against me later. No thank you to anyone who has said I'm too loud. No thank you to men who don't see me as a person, but as an object that another man owns. No thank you to employers that exploit every ounce of labor they can without paying for it. No thank you to landlords. No thank you to adults that make fun of children. No thank you to those that lost their sense of whimsy, so try to shame me out of mine. No thank you to people who don't use their blinkers. No thank you to any man, ever, that has called me dumb. No thank you to anyone who told me to find my niche and stay there. No thank you to those that invite me to dinner, but never my friends.

No thank you, no thank you, no thank you.

Insincere Sincerity

I plant words in gardens with the best of intentions,

But can't stop the harvest from rotting.

I sneeze out thoughts to be met with insincere blessings.

I cut and paste words to printer paper like a ransom note,

Call it a book, and let the hostages go.

I listen to my heartbeat match the drums I play,

Then rip it out of my chest, Temple of Doom style.

My heart would never betray me like I would betray it.

I have bone meal and tissues and words

Have weight and they mean things.

(You cannot ignore the tantrums of the child and be surprised by the wrath of the woman.)

The Troll that Lives Under My Brain
Part Two

My riddle three holds the key,

It will set you free, to a degree.

The fable is playful but still enabled

Those unstable to become fatal.

Alas, the forecast can't surpass

The sass that begins to harass.

The only thinker becomes a drinker,

Hook, line, and sinker.

The emotion is an ocean moving in slow motion

The commotion of devotion and a demotion.

Intend to defend any old friend

Please comprehend; this isn't the end

A black cat and crooked hat come with chitchat,

Wild wombats and all that.

Widespread, all red bloodshed

Look ahead, a warhead fueled by dread.

The makeover hangover,

Leftover pushover in a rover

Anyway, I pray for the stray blue Jay,

Decay, Broadway, go away.

The end of this book,

Say goodbye to the crook.

It's been fun, but I'm done,

And prepared to be shunned.

About the Author:

Samantha has been writing for the vast majority of her life, having her first poem published in elementary school. Her biggest loves are fantasy, dystopian, and poetry. When she isn't writing, she can be found curled up on a couch with her boyfriend. She also adores spending time with her god-son, Killian.

If you enjoyed this book, please leave a review online!

You can keep up to date with Samantha and her work at SamanthaNicklaus.com

www.ingramcontent.com/pod-product-compliance
Lightning Source LLC
Chambersburg PA
CBHW071933020426
42331CB00010B/2845